READING FLUENCY PASSAGES for 3rd GRADE with COMPREHENSION

Read the story 3 times. Circle the number each time you read it: **1 2 3**

The Candy Bowl

Abby loved to prank her family. Today she took a bunch of colorful candy pieces and mixed them all in one bowl. The candy pieces were all jumbled up. There were sweet, sour, and chocolate ones. However, no one was passing by the candy bowl. Abby was disappointed. She had expected everyone to try a handful right away. Abby had to work harder to make this prank successful. She grabbed the candy bowl and approached each family member. Now everyone took a handful. They all were shocked as they started to chew the candy. Abby started to giggle. That's when her entire family knew what she'd done. They'd been pranked, again!

1. What was Abby's prank this time?
_____
_____
_____

2. Why was Abby disappointed?
_____
_____
_____

3. How did Abby make it successful?
_____
_____
_____

4. What happened when Abby giggled?
_____
_____
_____

© Literacy with Aylin Claahsen 2024. All rights reserved.

© Literacy with Aylin Claahsen 2024. All rights reserved.

No part of this publication may be reproduced, distributed, or transmitted in any form or by any means. This includes photocopying, recording, or other electronic or mechanical methods without prior permission of the publisher, except in the case of brief quotations embodied in critical reviews and other noncommercial uses permitted by copyright law.

No part of this product maybe used or reproduced for commercial use.

Contact the author :
literacywithaylinclaahsen.com

Table of Contents	Page
The Candy Bowl	6-7
Cracked the Case	8-9
A Rough Start	10-11
Careless	12-13
The Coast	14-15
Traffic Signals	16-17
Slip and Fall	18-19
The Chase	20-21
Cheering Crew	22-23
Volunteer	24-25
Broken Toys	26-27
A New Team	28-29
Sunshine	30-31
Long Sleeves	32-33
Higher	34-35
Answer Keys for Questions	37-39

Instructions for Use

The main purpose of this pack is to help students develop their fluent reading skills. They will do this by completing repeated readings of each passage. Each passage will be followed up with responding to written comprehension questions.

Each Passage:
The student will read each passage three times. Each time the passage is read, the student will circle one of the numbers at the top of the page, until all three readings are complete.

Comprehension Questions:
Each passage comes with its own set of comprehension questions. After the student has read through the text three times, they can write their answers to the comprehension questions.

Answer Keys:
Answer Keys for the comprehension questions are included at the end. You can use these to check the student answered the questions correctly.

Read the story 3 times. Circle the number each time you read it: **1 2 3**

The Candy Bowl

Abby loved to prank her family. Today she took a bunch of colorful candy pieces and mixed them all in one bowl. The candy pieces were all jumbled up. There were sweet, sour, and chocolate ones. However, no one was passing by the candy bowl. Abby was disappointed. She had expected everyone to try a handful right away. Abby had to work harder to make this prank successful. She grabbed the candy bowl and approached each family member. Now everyone took a handful. They all were shocked as they started to chew the candy. Abby started to giggle. That's when her entire family knew what she'd done. They'd been pranked, again!

1. What was Abby's prank this time?

_____

_____

_____

2. Why was Abby disappointed?

_____

_____

_____

3. How did Abby make it successful?

_____

_____

_____

4. What happened when Abby giggled?

_____

_____

_____

Read the story 3 times. Circle the number each time you read it: 1   2   3

Cracked the Case

Alonso didn't know what was up with his sister. He kept trying to talk to Mora but she just kept snapping at him. She only wanted to argue, it seemed. Alonso was unsure what he did to cause her anger. So, he went to the kitchen to grab a snack. He planned to just spend some time on his own. However, once he sat down with his snack, Mora approached the table. She peered down at his snack. That's when Alonso knew what was wrong. Mora was hungry! Alonso pushed the snack toward Mora. She began eating right away and then smiled at Alonso. He was so glad he finally cracked the case!

1. How was Mora responding to Alonso?

_____

_____

_____

2. Why did Alonso go to the kitchen?

_____

_____

_____

3. What did Alonso figure out?

_____

_____

_____

4. How did Alonso help Mora?

_____

_____

_____

© Literacy with Aylin Claahsen 2024- present. All rights reserved.

Read the story 3 times. Circle the number each time you read it: 1   2   3

A Rough Start

I shuddered thinking about how my day started. It was our warmest day of winter. I was thrilled to have the chance to go outside without a puffy coat. I ran out to the front yard, but ended up not making it far. I slipped on some thin ice that I hadn't noticed. Falling right down, I hit the edge of the sidewalk. Pain shot up my leg. So I sat there howling until my dad came to check on me. He found me shivering from being on the ground. He saw that I was in major pain. My dad carried me inside and took care of me. It was a rough start to the day.

1. Why did the kid shudder?

_____

_____

_____

2. What was the kid thrilled about?

_____

_____

_____

3. Why didn't the kid make it far?

_____

_____

_____

4. How did the dad help the kid?

_____

_____

_____

Read the story 3 times. Circle the number each time you read it: **1 2 3**

Careless

Amani left school in a rush. Her shoelace was untied but she didn't let it bother her. Amani had to beat her brother home. If she didn't, Koda would end up eating their last peanut butter chocolate dessert. There was no way she'd let that happen. She could hear Koda shouting to her, but she ignored him. Reaching their driveway, she hurried inside. That's when she noticed her backpack was wide open. The only thing that remained was her laptop. Moments later, Koda ran up with everything from her bag. It was so kind of him after she had been so careless. Amani decided that she'd split the dessert with him, after all.

1. Why did Amani leave school in a rush?

_____

_____

_____

2. What did Amani notice when she got home?

_____

_____

_____

3. Why had Koda been shouting to Amani?

_____

_____

_____

4. Why did Amani decide to split the dessert?

_____

_____

_____

The Coast

Getting to visit the coast was a dream come true. Manny had never been but always wanted to go. His parents had set up a scavenger hunt for him to discover where they were headed on their trip. It took a lot of steps before he got to the final clue. But as he solved each one, Manny had a feeling he knew what the last clue would reveal. As soon as he opened the box he saw a clear image of the ocean. His parents explained that they'd drive up and down the coast this summer. It made Manny grin from ear to ear. He began a countdown. Manny couldn't wait for summer!

1. What was a dream come true for Manny?

_____

_____

_____

2. What did his parents set up?

_____

_____

_____

3. What did Manny see for the last clue?

_____

_____

_____

4. Why did Manny grin from ear to ear?

_____

_____

_____

Read the story 3 times. Circle the number each time you read it: 1   2   3

Traffic Signals

The walk signal continued to flash. Aditi stayed on her skateboard and sailed across the crosswalk. At the next block, Aditi saw the countdown for the walk signal dwindle. She paused on her skateboard. Aditi knew better than to risk trying to cross the street. Her parents always were hollering "safety first" as she headed out the door. She knew if she got hurt on her skateboard there was no chance they'd let her take it to school any longer. So, Aditi took their advice and always followed the traffic signals. She was hopeful this would continue to keep her safe on her skateboard! She liked it better than walking, after all.

1. What did Aditi see at the second crosswalk?

___

___

___

2. Why didn't Aditi risk crossing the street?

___

___

___

3. What did her parents always holler?

___

___

___

4. How would Aditi stay safe?

___

___

___

Read the story 3 times. Circle the number each time you read it: **1   2   3**

Slip and Fall

I reread the invite multiple times. The details of the event were still unclear to me. We needed to dress warm and be ready to slip and fall. The party would be outside. I wasn't super thrilled to read that part. But I was looking forward to seeing my friends. The day of the party, my mom dropped me off at an outdoor ice skating rink. We all grabbed ice skates, laced up, and instantly were wobbly. I was thankful when the instructor started a lesson. It was so helpful and made the rest of the party enjoyable! As the invite had warned, we did all slip and fall quite a bit.

1. What wasn't the kid thrilled to read?

_____

_____

_____

2. Where did the mom drop the kid off?

_____

_____

_____

3. Why was the kid thankful for the lesson?

_____

_____

_____

4. What happened quite a bit?

_____

_____

_____

Read the story 3 times. Circle the number each time you read it: **1   2   3**

The Chase

Hugo sat on his doorstep waiting for Luis. He kept checking his watch wondering why Luis wasn't there yet. Finally Hugo saw Luis coming down his street. Luis was riding his bike quickly. He almost crashed on Hugo's lawn as he came to an abrupt stop. Luis ran up to Hugo, out of breath. He then yanked Hugo inside. Once Luis stopped panting, he explained what happened. A giant dog was running loose by Luis's house. Since he was already on his bike, Luis offered to help the owner chase after the dog. But then the dog started chasing Luis. He got scared and darted off toward Hugo's house. Luis was so grateful to now be safe inside Hugo's house!

© Literacy with Aylin Claahsen 2024- present. All rights reserved.

1. Why did Hugo keep checking his watch?

_____

_____

_____

2. What happened when Luis arrived?

_____

_____

_____

3. Why was Luis so out of breath?

_____

_____

_____

4. Why was Luis grateful to be inside?

_____

_____

_____

Read the story 3 times. Circle the number each time you read it: 1   2   3

Cheering Crew

Basketball was my favorite sport to play. I love the game and I was also a great player. My coach explained that we had a bonus game coming up this weekend. He told us to invite anyone we wanted to the game. My coach said a big cheering crew would be helpful for this game. I wanted to invite my teacher and friends to the basketball game. But, whenever I was about to bring it up, my hands would start sweating. I didn't understand why I was so nervous to ask them. However, once I finally worked up the courage, I was thrilled to see how excited they all were. I'd have the best cheering crew in the stands!

1. What was coming up that weekend?

_____

_____

_____

2. What did the coach say would be helpful?

_____

_____

_____

3. Why did his hands start sweating?

_____

_____

_____

4. Why was he thrilled in the end?

_____

_____

_____

Read the story 3 times. Circle the number each time you read it: **1 2 3**

Volunteer

The animal shelter was packed full of animals in every single crate or cage. But, it was empty too, with no people looking to take home any animals. The lack of people made Jillian sad. She begged her dad to take all of the animals home. Jillian tried hard to persuade her dad but got nowhere. The clerk at the shelter overheard Jillian. She told them she had a better idea they might be able to agree on. The clerk suggested Jillian volunteer at the shelter twice a week to help out. Turning with pleading eyes to her dad, Jillian could see from the twinkle in his eyes that he was going to say yes. Jillian couldn't wait to start!

1. How was the animal shelter full and empty at the same time?

_____

_____

_____

2. What did Jillian beg her dad to do?

_____

_____

_____

3. What did the clerk suggest?

_____

_____

_____

4. How did Jillian know her dad would say yes?

_____

_____

_____

Read the story 3 times. Circle the number each time you read it: 1   2   3

Broken Toys

Caleb selected toys for his cousins. He chose ones that were unbreakable. His cousins were very rough with each other and with toys whenever they came over. Caleb didn't want any broken toys. The doorbell rang and as soon as his mom opened the door, his cousins charged down the hall. They headed straight for the basement. While Caleb tried his hardest to get them to play with the softer toys he'd chosen, he had zero luck. Within just a few seconds, his cousins were being the opposite of gentle. They were fighting and tackling one another. Caleb's aunt hurried downstairs and pulled them apart. She then sent them outside to play where they couldn't break anything.

1. Why was Caleb selecting toys?

_____

_____

_____

2. What happened when the door was opened?

_____

_____

_____

3. How did the cousins act in the basement?

_____

_____

_____

4. How did his aunt solve the problem?

_____

_____

_____

Read the story 3 times. Circle the number each time you read it: **1   2   3**

A New Team

Tanisha didn't recognize anyone on her new team. She hoped to be with her former teammates, but it wasn't the case. Tanisha couldn't understand how she was with a totally new team of soccer players. Something didn't seem right. She stood on the field listening for her name as the new coach went through the roster. The coach was nearing the end of the list. That was when Tanisha heard her name called, but it was coming from the opposite side of the field. Tanisha turned toward that group. That's when she realized she was on the wrong end of the field. Relief flooded over Tanisha as she raced to the right spot with her former teammates.

1. What had Tanisha hoped for?

_____

_____

_____

2. What couldn't Tanisha understand?

_____

_____

_____

3. Where did Tanisha hear her name?

_____

_____

_____

4. Why did relief flood over Tanisha?

_____

_____

_____

Read the story 3 times. Circle the number each time you read it: **1   2   3**

Sunshine

It was a pleasant day outside. The sun was shining bright and it was drying up all the puddles. Rain had fallen for multiple days in a row. Tobias has been stuck inside with his sister for too many days. The sun felt wonderful and boosted their moods. Tobias spent the day riding his bike all over the trails by his house. While they had been sick of each other, his sister ended up joining him for the bike rides. On one of their rides they stopped to look at the large pond. That's when they discovered a beaver in the water. The beaver entertained them for a while. It seemed like even the beaver liked the sunshine!

1. Why was it such a pleasant day?

_____

_____

_____

2. What had the rain forced Tobias and his sister to do?

_____

_____

_____

3. How did Tobias and his sister spend the day?

_____

_____

_____

4. What did they discover on their rides?

_____

_____

_____

Read the story 3 times. Circle the number each time you read it: **1   2   3**

Long Sleeves

I liked to play with my cat, but I learned my lesson last time. My cat liked to play with a little feather that hung from a string. I would dangle the string in front of her and then pull it away as she reached for it. Sometimes she'd be quick enough to grab the feather. Other times I'd pull it back quicker than she could move. But last time, I wasn't wearing long sleeves and her claws caught my arm instead of the feather. I ended up with giant scratches on my arm. It was painful, but I know she wasn't trying to hurt me. From now on I just wore long sleeves to protect myself when we played!

1. What toy did her cat like?

_____

_____

_____

2. What would happen when she dangled the string?

_____

_____

_____

3. What problem happened the last time?

_____

_____

_____

4. How did the girl solve the problem?

_____

_____

_____

Higher

Kayla kept climbing up higher and higher. She didn't turn around once. Kayla was nervous that she'd get scared of how high she'd gone if she looked back. She knew her dad was right behind her since he had been talking nonstop their whole trip up the mountain. The higher they got the more rocks there seemed to be so she was extra careful. Her dad told her they were almost at the top where they'd take a break. Kayla was relieved. They made it to a large clearing. That's when Kayla stumbled. It was like her feet could no longer keep moving. She was grateful to be in an open field where she couldn't tumble down!

1. Why didn't Kayla ever turn around?

_____

_____

_____

2. How did she know her dad was still right behind her?

_____

_____

_____

3. What happened when they got to the top?

_____

_____

_____

4. Why was Kayla grateful for the open field?

_____

_____

_____

Answer Key

You can use these to check the written answers to each comprehension question.

Story Title	Question 1	Question 2	Question 3	Question 4
The Candy Bowl	Abby's prank was putting a bunch of different kinds of candy in one bowl, mixed up.	Abby was disappointed because no one was passing by the bowl to try the candy.	Abby grabbed the candy bowl and brought it around to everyone to try.	Once Abby giggled her family knew she'd pranked them again.
Cracked the Case	Mora kept snapping at Alonso.	Alonso went to the kitchen to spend some time on his own.	Alonso figured out that Mora was just hungry.	Alonso let Mora have his snack to help her.
A Rough Start	He shuddered as he thought about the start to his day.	He was thrilled the weather was nice and he didn't have to wear his big puffy coat.	He didn't make it far because he slipped on thin ice and hurt himself.	His dad carried him inside and took care of him.
Careless	Amani left school in a rush so she could beat her brother home to get the last peanut butter chocolate dessert.	Amani noticed that her backpack had been wide open and most things fell out.	Koda had been shouting to Amani trying to get her to notice her stuff falling out.	Amani thought it was so kind of Koda to help her when she was being careless.
The Coast	Being able to visit the coast was a dream come true for Manny.	His parents set up a scavenger hunt for him to find out where they were going.	Manny saw a clear image of the ocean.	He was looking forward to his trip.

© Literacy with Aylin Claahsen 2024- present. All rights reserved.

Answer Key

You can use these to check the written answers to each comprehension question.

Story Title	Question 1	Question 2	Question 3	Question 4
Traffic Signals	Aditi saw the walk signal dwindling.	Aditi wanted to be safe so her parents would still let her skateboard to school.	Her parents always hollered "safety first".	Aditi took their advice and always followed the traffic signals.
Slip and Fall	The kid wasn't thrilled that the party would be held outside in the cold.	The mom dropped the kid off at the outdoor ice skating rink.	The kid liked the lesson because it was helpful and made the rest of the party enjoyable.	Everyone slipped and fell a lot.
The Chase	Hugo kept checking his watch as he waited for Luis to show up.	Luis ran up to Hugo, out of breath, and yanked him inside the house.	Luis was out of breath because a giant dog had been chasing him.	He was grateful to be safe inside where the dog couldn't get him.
Cheering Crew	A bonus basketball game was coming up that weekend.	The coach said it would be helpful to have a big cheering crew.	His hands were sweating because he was nervous to ask his friends and teacher to come watch him.	He was thrilled to see how excited everyone was to come cheer for him.
Volunteer	The animal shelter was full of animals, but empty of people who wanted to take the pets home.	Jillian begged her dad to take the animals home with them.	The clerk suggested Jillian volunteer at the shelter twice a week to help out.	Jillian knew he dad would say yes because of the twinkle in his eye.

© Literacy with Aylin Claahsen 2024- present. All rights reserved.

Answer Key

You can use these to check the written answers to each comprehension question.

Story Title	Question 1	Question 2	Question 3	Question 4
Broken Toys	Caleb was trying to find toys his cousins wouldn't break.	His cousins charged down the hall and headed straight to the basement as soon as they got inside.	The cousins were the opposite of gentle. They were fighting and tackling each other.	His aunt pulled the cousins apart and sent them outside to play.
A New Team	Tanisha had hoped to be on a team with her former teammates, again.	Tanisha couldn't understand how she was on a team with all new players.	Tanisha heard her name from the opposite side of the field.	Relief flooded over Tanisha when she realized she was just in the wrong spot.
Sunshine	It was a pleasant day because the sun was shining bright and drying up the puddles.	The rain had made Tobias and his sister spend too much time inside, together.	They spent the day riding their bikes.	They found a beaver in the large pond.
Long Sleeves	Her cat liked a toy that had a feather hanging from a string.	Her cat would try to get the feather when they girl pulled it away.	Last time the cat's claws had scratched the kid's arm.	The kid now always wore long sleeves when they played with this toy.
Higher	Kayla didn't turn around because she didn't want to get scared with how high they'd gone.	She knew her dad was there the entire time because he talked nonstop.	Kayla stumbled when they got to the open field because her feet could no longer move.	She was grateful to stumble in the open field because she couldn't tumble down.

© Literacy with Aylin Claahsen 2024- present. All rights reserved.

Copyrighted Materials: All Rights Reserved
© Literacy with Aylin Claahsen 2024

Terms of Use

This resource is for personal use/single classroom use only. Placing any part of this product on the Internet (including classroom, school or district websites) is prohibited by the Digital Millennium Copyright Act (DMCA).

literacywithaylinclaahsen.com

Scan the QR code to follow me on Instagram for more ideas!

Made in the USA
Columbia, SC
03 September 2024